INFORMATION
SYSTEMS
workbook ≪

Lejla Vrazalic
University of Wollongong

Joseph Meloche
University of Wollongong

WILEY
John Wiley & Sons Australia, Ltd

First published 2005 by
John Wiley & Sons Australia, Ltd
33 Park Road, Milton, Qld 4064

Offices also in Sydney and Melbourne

ISBN 0 470 80803 9

Cover design images: © Digital Vision

Printed in Singapore by
CMO Image Printing Enterprise

10 9 8 7 6 5 4 3 2 1

Contents

Introduction

An Overview

This workbook is intended for use in an Information Systems course at an introductory level. It has been developed primarily for the needs of tertiary students studying Information Systems (IS) or Information Technology (IT) in Australian universities. As such, the workbook has been designed to be used in structured two-hour tutorials, rather than as a stand-alone textbook for an entire IS course. The contents of this workbook are intended to complement a standard Introduction to IS/IT textbook. While a textbook may be used to present key IS/IT concepts in lectures, this workbook consists of project-based modules and activities intended to demonstrate how these concepts are applied in practice.

Structure of this workbook

The workbook consists of five modules. Each module is related to a relevant set of IS/IT concepts which students are required to apply using a project-based approach and appropriate software tools. However, these software tools are not the primary concern of the workbook, and as such they are not described specifically. The focus is on applying IS/IT concepts in practice.

The five modules that make up the workbook are as follows:

Module 1	Project Management
Module 2	IS/IT Infrastructure Plan
Module 3	Organisational Database
Module 4	Web-based Information System
Module 5	IS/IT Management Plan

The modules are related and each module consists of a set of tasks and activities that students should work on in teams during a tutorial. At the end of each module, the team is required to demonstrate their understanding of the relevant IS/IT concepts by producing a report or similar output and submitting it to their lecturer and/or tutor for assessment. The outcomes of each module are based on the activities for that module.

All of the outcomes are related to a specific project. There are five project briefs to choose from at the end of this section. Each project brief contains a description of an organisation that is a small business, including a book festival organiser, a café, a health club, a business consultancy, and a resort. Each team must select one project brief to use in completing all of the five modules. The project briefs contain most of the information students need to complete the modules. However, where students believe the information to be incomplete, they can make any assumptions, providing they are not in conflict with the chosen project brief. These assumptions should be stated clearly as part of the outcomes for each module shown above.

At the end of each module, students are also asked to reflect on their learning experience. These reflections are then summarised in the conclusion and presented to the class.

Project Briefs

Books 4 Life

Mission and Goals

Books 4 Life is an event organiser that organises the Annual Fraser Island Book Festival. The Festival celebrates the country's rich literary heritage and encourages people of all ages to read more and read widely. The goals of Books 4 Life and the Festival include:

- To provide public programs about books, writing, and reading for people of all ages.
- To encourage use of the resources provided by libraries.
- To foster knowledge of local authors and to encourage children to write through reading and discussion of their reading and writing efforts.
- To promote an appreciation of local literature and to develop life-long education skills through reading, writing and discussion.
- To cultivate the habits of families reading and discussion of the stories they read and write.
- To increase access to books and knowledge by offering reasonable prices and discounts for students and academics.
- To provide books in other languages to cater for customers whose first language is not English.

Main Business of the Organisation

The Book Festival is an annual international event. It aims to highlight Australian writing and to present it to the international community. Thus it is a forum for Australian writers' publishers and distributors. It also gives Australians access to some of the best and most recent international publications with over one hundred countries represented at last year's event.

It also showcases Australia through the pristine environment of Fraser Island, the world's largest sand island, on the world's only island continent, Australia. The Fraser Island Book Festival showcases local heritage and activities that promote tourism are featured.

The festival occurs during the whale watching season and packages are available in association with local resorts and travel agencies, which Books 4 Life handles. This year the Blue Coral Resort is a major sponsor. The Festival is growing every year. There were more than 1000 participants in 2004, which is a 12% growth over 2003.

Staff

Manager
Administrative staff
Marketing and Promotions staff
Financial operations staff
Sponsorships co-ordninator

Current IT Infrastructure

Books 4 Life is currently housed in a small office where staff work on a part-time basis and share 3 mid-range desktop computers. Only two of the computers have MS Office 97 installed, while the third is used mainly for accounting and financial activities. One computer is connected to the Internet to avoid hackers breaking into the database of festival participants. The Manager is a skilled IT user who knows how to write Java programs.

Stanwell Park Café

Mission and Goals

The Stanwell Park Café aims to provide people with a place to meet with friends. The Café is located in a seaside setting perched high on the cliffs of Stanwell Park. While the town itself is small the Café seeks to provide locals and travellers with a comfortable place to meet and eat in a setting complemented by the natural beauty of the region. The Café offers local food based on seasonal availability and choice fresh fish and seafood. The Café also provides a small gallery for local artists to display their work in an effort to foster artistic development in the area. The goals of Stanwell Park Café include:

- To provide a comfortable place for local and travelers alike to visit.
- To provide local and seasonal food and beverages for a sensible price.
- To create a modern relaxed environment that encourages people to congregate and socialise.
- To foster artistic talent by inviting local artists to display their work.
- To offer variety in the food and beverages served to guests.

Main Business of the Organisation

The Stanwell Park Café is as small local café. It is set in a seaside setting perched high on the cliffs of Stanwell Park. Its modern décor and intimate settings makes it the perfect setting for small groups and couples to meet for meals/drinks and conversation.

With quality chefs and kitchen staff, Stanwell Park Café offers excellent quality and choice of food that is certain to satisfy. The venue is also used as a gallery for local artists to display their works for the public to see and purchase. The Café sells the art works on behalf of the local artists and takes a commission of 2% per sale.

Due to increasing tourist numbers, the café is becoming very popular and in 6 months the owner will expand into a neighbouring shop which has closed down. This will allow seating for an additional 40 to 60 people and more staff will have to be hired.

Staff

Café Manager (also the owner)
Chef and kitchen staff
Waiters and waitresses
Administrative assistant
Part-time accountant

Current IT Infrastructure

Stanwell Park Café currently doesn't have much space for computer equipment because of seating arrangements. Waiters and waitresses use a pen and paper system, and the cashier isn't connected to the kitchen inventory so the chef has to manually count at the end of each day the stock left. The accountant brings in his own laptop to the café, while the administrative assistant (who takes care of the art works that are for sale and other paperwork) maintains manual records of art sales and payments to artists. The administrative assistant has some previous experience with developing websites.

W Beauty, Health & Fitness Club

Mission and Goals

The W Beauty, Health & Fitness Club aims to encourage and motivate people to strive for healthy living by providing fitness facilities and activities for all ages and fitness levels. It aims to provide fitness programs in a comfortable spa like environment and provides the opportunity for people to follow fitness plans that are tailored to their individual needs. It provides members with individual health assessment, a full range of spa treatments and advice for healthy living. The goals of W Beauty, Health & Fitness Club include:

- To provide excellent service to all members.
- To provide a friendly environment that is pleasant for members.
- To provide personal advice to members about the best exercise regime for them.
- To encourage participation in team activities and competitions run by the gym.
- To provide the most up-to-date training equipment and advice for members on how to maximise the benefits available from the equipment and services provided.
- To provide members with a complete fitness health and spa experience.

Main Business of the Organisation

Fitness is for everyone and everywhere. The W Beauty, Health & Fitness Club is located a central and accessible location, which offers everyone, no matter what their size, shape or ability level, the opportunity to improve his or her health and fitness and the opportunity to have fun. Upon entering the Club guests will notice a difference, in the comfortable surroundings, inspiring images, friendly staff, and the service provided by the professional trainers, helpful instructors and therapists. The members have access to the latest in developments in programs and equipment. W Beauty, Health & Fitness Club is dedicated to ensuring each member has an exceptional experience on every visit to the club.

W Beauty, Health & Fitness Club strives to provide the members with more than just a place to get fit. They'll be amazed at the added benefits of being a Beauty Fitness Club member.

Opened only two years ago, recently the Club enrolled its 2000th member! With increasing numbers, the owners are increasingly worried about the business operations. As the business grows it will be necessary to make changes to the procedures and infrastructure. The Owners do a lot of traveling every year to find out what the latest trends are worldwide.

Staff

Two owners
Club manager
Administrative staff
Accountant
Marketing co-ordinator
Personal trainers, instructors and therapists

Current IT Infrastructure

Up until recently, the Club had coped with having four desktop computers to do their work – two at the front desk and two in the "back room". However, the queues are getting longer and customers are no longer happy to wait! They don't understand why they have to go to the desk every time they come for a visit instead of just scanning their cards and walking through. The marketing co-ordinator used to work for an IT company and developed some of their systems in Java.

Modern Marketing Consultants

Mission and Goals

Modern Marketing Consultants aims to provide consulting services in all areas of modern business and to find new and creative ways to market business products and services. They provide business startup advice and small business advice as well as business strategies, for large and multi-national businesses.

Modern's business consultants provide sound business advice based on extensive real world business experience and knowledge. They are one of the few consulting firms that offer consulting in all areas of business. Their slogan is "Our ability to keep your business ahead of the pack will help your bottom line". The goals of Modern Marketing Consultants include:

- To provide excellent service to all clients.
- To provide strategic advice
- To know their clients' business and their market needs
- To communicate clients' attributes to the specific markets in an efficient manner
- To grow clients' business
- To ensure that clients' outperform your competitors
- To increase clients' competitive advantage
- To maximise clients' opportunities and benefits

Main Business of the Organisation

The main business areas are: research, planning and training and seminars.

Research

Modern provides qualitative and quantitative research to help clients find the proper solutions for their business.

Planning

Modern provides business planning in all areas of business to help assure clients' business success. They create simple effective business plans and growth strategies. They have teams that can implement business strategies in an effective manner.

Training And Seminars

Modern provides training in all aspects of business and comprehensive business seminars.

Staff

Owner/Manager
Administrative staff
Research co-ordinator and staff
Training co-ordinator and staff
Planning co-ordinator and staff
Marketing co-ordinator
Accountant

Current IT Infrastructure

Modern's client base is growing all the time and they need to upgrade their computer network which currently consists of seven desktop computers and one laptop. The owner was an IT consultant before opening Modern and is an expert computer user.

Blue Coral Resort

Mission and Goals

The Blue Coral Resort's mission is to provide a unique Ecotourism experience in a native environment in which city dwellers and international travelers can come and escape for a holiday. They aim to provide a high level of service and excellent amenities to make each guest's stay as pleasurable, educational and interesting as possible. Being on the Great Barrier Reef they want their guests to enjoy all that the reef has to offer and to promote themselves as a responsible Ecotourism provider. The goals of Blue Coral include:

- To attract a wide range of guests to the Blue Coral Resort
- To maintain a high standard of service
- To promote local attractions to guests in an effort to support the local tourism industry
- To provide employment to local people and work towards their hospitality training.
- To maintain customer satisfaction.
- To strive towards excellence in all aspects of the business.
- To provide locals with a great place to experience the reef.
- To look towards expanding in years to come as the demand for accommodation increases in an environmental sensitive manner.
- To promote the Ecotourism industry and encourage responsible development.

Main Business of the Organisation

The Blue Coral Resort is an environmental tourist establishment set in the Gateway to the Great Barrier Reef in Southeast Queensland one hour from the historic town of Bundaberg. Its tranquil setting makes it the perfect place for people to come and experience a natural marine environment. It is suitable for individuals, couples and families and has many great activities on offer both on site and in the local area. The Blue Coral Resort features hotel comforts and has a small restaurant, which provides breakfasts for each guest each morning made from local produce and delightful seafood meals. The Blue Coral Resort also offers many package deals for guests and also caters for small corporate clients. It has whale-watching tours, as the Humpback whales pass close to resort. It also provides for night trips to nearby Mon Repos beach where some special marine visitors have established Australia's largest and most accessible turtle rookery. Loggerhead, green, leatherback and flatback turtles come ashore from November to February to lay eggs.

The Resort has just added an extra wing of six rooms to the existing twelve rooms with sea views. They are fully booked out eight months in advance.

Staff

Manager
Administrative staff
Receptionist
Concierge
Cleaners
Promotions and marketing co ordinator

Current IT Infrastructure

Blue Coral has three computers at the reception and two more in the offices. There are also two laptops that are used as needed by various staff. Many guests have asked about Internet access but the Resort doesn't offer any at the moment.

Module 1

Project Management

Relevant lecture content	Project management
Relevant textbook chapter(s)	
Due date	

Introduction

This module relates to project management issues and concepts. In the Introduction you were provided with five project briefs. As part of this module you will be required to form a project team, select one of the five projects and develop a plan for managing and monitoring your chosen project.

Here is an outline of the tasks for this module:
- Form a project team and outline each team member's expertise
- Select a project manager and an assistant project manager
- Develop a project schedule
- Create a set of communication and co-ordination procedures for your team.

You may be required to use project management software as part of this module. Your lecturer and/or tutor will give you more information about this.

This module is very important because it contains information that you will require to complete your project. It represents the "blueprint" for your project and you should refer to it in order to ensure that your project is on track. At the end of this module, you will be required to develop and submit a **Project Management** report based on your work.

Project Team

The success of your project will largely depend on the dedication of your team members. High performance teams that achieve results do not only have all the right skills, but are also prepared to commit themselves to success from the outset.

In real life, you often won't be in a position to choose your own team. Instead, your supervisor will assign you to a team and you may end up working closely with individuals that you don't know. Another important aspect of teamwork is building relationships with your team members.

You will be working as part of a team for the rest of the semester. The team will consist of you and your classmates. You probably don't know everyone in your class, so to succeed you will have to make a commitment to your team and build relationships with your team members.

Activity 1.1

Talk to your classmates and form a project team consisting of three or four individuals. Give your team a name and, if you wish, design a logo or slogan for your team.

When you have formed a team, write down all your team members' names and contact details in the space below.

Name	E-mail address	Phone number

The next step involves getting to know your team members. To work effectively, it is important to capitalise on the strengths and expertise of each individual member. You may find that your team members often have complementary skills. For example, while some are good at report writing, others may be good at doing presentations. This also means that team members can learn skills from each other and improve any areas of weakness.

Activity 1.2

Find out what your team members are good at and what they can contribute to the project. Each team member should address the following questions:
1. What are three things that you are good at?
2. What is an area of weakness that you would like to improve?

Here are some suggested responses to assist you (but you will probably think of others!):
- Prioritising tasks
- Organising tasks
- Writing essays/reports
- Doing research
- Using word processing software
- Proofreading
- Presenting
- Finding creative solutions
- Planning
- Solving problems
- Resolving conflicts

After you have finished discussing your teams' strengths and weaknesses, write down the responses in the space below. You can refer back to this section when you are allocating tasks at later stages in the project to ensure the best fit between the individual and the task.

Name	Strengths	Weaknesses

Project Manager

Every project has a project manager. The project manager is responsible for leading the team through the steps in the project management process. The project manager must, therefore, have strong leadership skills as well as the ability to co-ordinate and organise the team so that they work together effectively and efficiently.

Your team needs to select a Project Manager. He or she will be responsible for the overall project. This role will involve overseeing different aspects of the project and ensuring that all the tasks are completed on time. It will also entail resolving and handling any problems that may arise in completing the tasks. In the previous activity you discussed the strengths and weaknesses of your individual team members. Based on your discussion, you will have to select a project manager for your team.

In real life, project managers may resign, or fall ill, or be prevented by some other circumstances from doing their job. This is why it is important to select an assistant project manager as well. The assistant project manager of your team will take over overall responsibility for the project, whenever the project manager is unable to.

Activity 1.3
Select a project manager and an assistant project manager for your team.

Write down the names of your project manager and assistant project manager below:

Project Manager	
Assistant Project Manager	

Project Schedule

The remaining four modules in this workbook relate to different aspects of your project. Each module requires you to complete a specific project task, as follows:

- Module 2: Prepare an IS/IT infrastructure plan
- Module 3: Develop a database for your organisation
- Module 4: Build a web-based information system for your organisation
- Module 5: Formulate a strategic IS/IT management plan

Your lecturer and/or tutor will have provided you with deadlines for each of the above tasks. Based on these deadlines, you have to develop a project schedule.

A project schedule is a planning document which indicates the tasks that have to be completed, when they have to be completed by, and by whom. The project schedule also usually contains information about resources that will be required to complete the tasks. (Refer to the relevant chapter in your textbook to find out more information about project schedules.)

Project schedules can also involve the preparation of Gantt charts or Program Evaluation and Review Technique (PERT) charts. These are project management techniques. Specialised project management software can be used to develop the Gantt and PERT charts. Your lecturer and/or tutor may demonstrate this type of software to you.

You will now be required to prepare a project schedule with your team members. In order to do this, you will need to have a basic understanding of what is involved in the remaining four modules. Read through modules 2 to 4 briefly before you begin preparing the project schedule. Remember that you are proposing a plan of action, at this stage only. The plan may change later when you find out more in-depth information about what is involved in each module. This is all part of monitoring the progress of a project and changes are inevitable, so you can adjust your project schedule afterward if required.

Activity 1.4

Based on the deadlines for each of the modules set by your lecturer and/or tutor, develop a project schedule for your team. Prepare a Gantt chart as part of the project schedule.

Here's what you should include:
1. Decompose the main project task in each module into smaller sub-tasks. For example, the IS/IT infrastructure plan involves hardware, software and network infrastructure. Based on this, you may choose to decompose the IS/IT infrastructure plan into three sub-tasks.
2. Allocate each task/sub-task to a team member and set a deadline for each one. Try to match tasks/sub-tasks to team members' individual strengths which you have identified previously.

3. It would also be useful to indicate what a team member should do once the task/sub-task is complete. For example, when one team member completes the hardware sub-task in the IS/IT infrastructure plan, he/she should send it to the project manager by e-mail.
4. List any resources that will be required to complete a task/sub-task. For example, when preparing the hardware sub-task in the IS/IT infrastructure plan, you may require access to the World Wide Web to search for appropriate hardware and prices.
5. Develop a "Plan B" or a contingency plan. Things may not work out as you planned. For example, one of your team members may fall ill. You should have a strategy in place to deal with such problems that may arise so that you can still meet your deadlines.

Communication and Co-ordination Procedures

The failure rate of information systems projects is very high. While there are a number of reasons for project failure, one of the most common is the lack of effective communication and co-ordination procedures. To work successfully, team members must communicate with each other and co-ordinate tasks so that there is no duplication or redundancy. This is why it is necessary to create communication and co-ordination procedures at the outset of a project.

When preparing communication and co-ordination procedures, the team members' needs and circumstances should be taken into account. For example, some team members may not have access to e-mail on a daily basis, while others may be unable to meet face-to-face regularly. There are a number of different communication and co-ordination strategies a team can employ to overcome these problems.

The final activity in this module involves preparing a set of communication and co-ordination procedures for your team.

Activity 1.5
Discuss different options with your team members that will ensure that you maintain effective communication and co-ordination at all times. For example, you may propose to meet at the library once every week, or you may suggest using an online group service such as Yahoo!™ groups to share files and exchange e-mails. After you have considered your options, prepare a set of communication and co-ordination procedures. This should include a detailed description of how you will maintain regular contact and co-ordinate tasks. You should also state how you propose to monitor the progress of your team and ensure that you are able to meet your deadlines.

Module 1 Outcome: Project Management Report

The activities in this module were designed to assist you with managing the project tasks in the following four modules. You should now have a project team and a project manager. You should also be aware of your team members' individual strengths and weaknesses. Finally, you should have a detailed plan for completing the project tasks in the subsequent modules and co-ordinating this process.

Compile **all** of the information that you prepared based on the above activities into a single **Project Management** report and hand it in to your lecturer and/or tutor by the due date. You should also ensure that every member of your team has a copy of this report for their reference.

Your lecturer and/or tutor will provide you with the marking criteria based on which your **Project Management** report will be marked. Make sure you write down this criteria in the space provided below.

Marking Criteria	Marks
TOTAL	**100**

Outstanding Issues

Do you have any questions that you would like to raise with your lecturer and/or tutor about the contents of this module? Use the space below to write them down.

Module 2

IS/IT Infrastructure Plan

Relevant lecture content	Hardware, Software and Networks
Relevant textbook chapter(s)	
Due date	

Introduction

This module relates to three components of an information system: hardware, software and networks. As part of this module you will be required to prepare an information systems/information technology infrastructure plan detailing the hardware, software and network requirements for your selected organisation, given a specific budget. You will also be required to examine different loans that the organisation cam apply for to fund the implementation of the IS/IT infrastructure plan.

Here is an outline of the tasks for this module:
- Recommend the hardware devices that the organisation should acquire,
- Recommend the software that the organisation should acquire,
- Recommend the network hardware and software,
- Determine the repayments on a loan taken out to finance the hardware and software purchase.

You may be required to use spreadsheet software as part of this module. Your lecturer and/or tutor will give you more information about this.

At the end of this module, you will be required to develop and submit an **IS/IT Infrastructure Plan** based on your work.

Hardware

Hardware consists of the physical components of information systems such as the central processing unit (CPU), input devices (e.g. mouse, keyboard, touchscreen), output devices (e.g. monitor, printer, speakers), storage devices, and networking devices (e.g. modem). Hardware devices also include mobile devices such as personal digital assistants (PDAs). When selecting the most appropriate hardware, it is important to ensure that the chosen devices suit the needs of the users and/or the activities for which they are intended. For example, an Administrative Assistant who performs tasks such as preparing documents and scheduling appointments will not require a computer with a high speed CPU. However, she/he may require a laser printer. In contrast, a Graphic Designer will need a sophisticated computer system with a special monitor and graphics card.

In addition to meeting the needs of the users and their activities, an organisation purchasing or leasing hardware must also ensure that it satisfies other criteria and constraints as well. For example, the organisation has to take into account the following:

- the cost of purchasing/leasing the hardware;
- the compatibility of the hardware with existing systems and software;
- the performance and reliability of the hardware;
- the reliability of the hardware supplier;
- the ability to upgrade the hardware;
- how widely the hardware is used;
- how easy it is to install and use/operate the hardware;
- the support provided by the hardware supplier (including maintenance and warranty).

Selecting the most appropriate hardware to purchase is not as simple as it may appear to be. It requires taking into account all of the above criteria, as well as sourcing information about the performance of the hardware, the hardware manufacturer and quotes from suppliers. Most of this information can be found on the World Wide Web. Discussion forums are particularly useful as a source of information because real users discuss their experiences with actual hardware that they have purchased and used.

One of the tasks in this module is to propose a hardware infrastructure for the organisation you have selected. Read the organisational brief again carefully, and based on the information provided complete the activity below with your project team.

Activity 2.1

Discuss the following questions with your project team. Where required, make assumptions about the organisation and/or the users if you do not have complete information.
1. What hardware infrastructure currently exists in the organisation?
2. Who are the users in the organisation and what does their work involve?
3. Based on your previous answer, what hardware devices do the users need to do their jobs?
4. Does the current hardware infrastructure meet the needs of the users?
5. What additional hardware devices, if any, do you propose the organisation should purchase/lease? You do not have to list the specifications, only the devices in general (e.g. a laptop, a laser printer and a digital camera).

After you have finished, write down the outcomes of your discussion in the space provided.

Existing hardware infrastructure

User	Description of work	Hardware needs

Assumptions

Summarise the outcome of your discussion below by listing the total number of hardware devices required.

Hardware	Total number required

You have now identified the hardware needs of the users in the organisation. However, the manager of your organisation only has **$12,000 to spend on both hardware and software**. Furthermore, the manager does not wish to spend large amounts of money on maintenance, and requires reliable hardware from an established supplier that will not be a drain on the organisation's resources, that will be compatible with the existing hardware and simple to install and use.

Activity 2.2

Taking into account what the manager has indicated above, discuss possible hardware devices that you could purchase for the organisation with your project team, keeping in mind the hardware needs of the users that you identified in Activity 2.1. You should use the World Wide Web to search for specific devices and the cost of purchasing or leasing these devices.

As you work through Activity 2.2, make a note of the hardware that you come across and that may be appropriate considering the users' needs and the manager's criteria and constraints. Also note the URL of any websites from where you sourced your information. Finally, justify why you have selected that particular hardware in relation to the users' needs and the manager's criteria.

URL:		
Device	**Specifications & Price**	**Justification**

URL:		
Device	**Specifications & Price**	**Justification**

URL:		
Device	**Specifications & Price**	**Justification**

URL:		
Device	**Specifications & Price**	**Justification**

URL:		
Device	**Specifications & Price**	**Justification**

URL:		
Device	**Specifications & Price**	**Justification**

URL:		
Device	**Specifications & Price**	**Justification**

You have now identified a set of possible hardware devices for your organisation. In the next section, you will consider the software needs of the organisation.

Software

Software consists of programs that control the operation of hardware. Software is generally classified into two types: systems software and applications software. Systems software coordinates the general operation of the hardware devices. It includes the operating system and system utilities for managing files, handling system errors, communicating with peripheral devices, etc. Most systems software is pre installed on a computer at the time of purchase/lease. Applications software is used to perform specific tasks and solve specific problems that users may have. For example, a word processor is applications software that is used to prepare documents, generate letters to clients, etc. Most applications software is sold individually, however, some is 'bundled' together into software suites that consist of a word processor, spreadsheet software and database software.

Software can be acquired in a variety of ways. Some generic software is best purchased 'off-the-shelf', while other software that is more specialised to the needs of the organisation, is best developed 'in-house'. Some software developers will customise their software to suit the needs of the organisation. Depending on how the software is acquired, the cost of the software will vary. Software developed 'in-house' may be expensive and time-consuming, however, some users may also have software development skills and may choose to develop software for themselves/ Software purchased 'off-the-shelf' will often require a number of licences. It is illegal to purchase one copy of a particular package (with a corresponding single-user license) and then install it on more than one computer. If there are four users in your organisation that require a word processor, it will be necessary to purchase four licences for the word processor. This may differ if the software is intended for use by groups ('groupware') or is freely available ('freeware'). Different software developers will have diverse licensing arrangements for their products, so it is important to read the Software License Agreement carefully, before installing any software.

Similarly to hardware, software should match the needs of the users. For example, the Administrative Assistant will require a word processor to prepare documents and calendar software to keep track of appointments, while the Graphics Designer will need desktop publishing software and a drawing package. The same criteria that applies to hardware, applies to software when making a decision about what to purchase/develop, including:

- the cost of purchasing/developing the software;
- the compatibility of the software with previous versions, and existing software and hardware;
- the performance and reliability of the software;
- the reliability of the software developer (if not developed 'in-house');
- the ability to upgrade the software;
- how widely the software is used;
- how easy it is to install and use/operate the software;
- the support provided by the software developed (including troubleshooting and technical assistance).

One of the tasks in this module is to propose software solutions for the organisation you have selected. Read the organisational brief again carefully, and based on the information provided complete the activity below with your project team.

Activity 2.3

Discuss the following questions with your project team. Where required, make assumptions about the organisation and/or the users if you do not have complete information.

1. What software is currently being used in the organisation?
2. Based on what you have discussed previously about the users in the organisation and their work, what software do the users need to do their jobs?
3. Does the current software meet the needs of the users?
4. What additional software, if any, do you propose the organisation should purchase/develop? You do not have to list the specifications, only the software in general (e.g. a word processor, a database software, an accounting software).

After you have finished, write down the outcomes of your discussion in the space provided.

Existing software infrastructure

User	Software needs

Assumptions

It has been mentioned previously that some users are also skilled in software development. If this is the case, it may be more appropriate and cheaper to ask such users to develop their own software.

Activity 2.4

Discuss with your project team whether there are any users in your organisation who have the skills to develop software that will meet the needs you have identified in Activity 2.3. Put an asterisk (*) next to those users in the previous table whom you consider to be skilled enough to do this.

Summarise the outcome of your discussion in the space below by listing the software requirements, whether you think the software should be purchased 'off-the-shelf', developed 'in-house' or customised. Where appropriate, you should also indicate the number of licences needed.

Software	Purchased/ Developed/ Customised	Number of licences (if applicable)

You have now identified the software needs of the users in the organisation and the number of software licences required. Remember that you have only **$12,000 to spend on both hardware and software**. Although the manager would like to save money, she/he does not wish to compromise the stability and integrity of the organisation's information systems. Therefore, only reliable software from established developers will be approved.

Activity 2.5

Taking into account what the manager has indicated above, discuss possible software that you could purchase/develop for the organisation with your project team, keeping in mind the software needs of the users that you identified in Activity 2.3, the hardware that you are considering purchasing/leasing (as per Activity 2.2) and the skills of the users in your organisation. You should use the World Wide Web to search for specific software and the cost of purchasing that software. Don't forget to purchase multiple licences where required.

As you work through Activity 2.5, make a note of the software that you come across and that may be appropriate considering the users' needs and the manager's criteria and constraints. Also note the URL of any websites from where you sourced your information. Finally, justify why you have selected that particular software in relation to the users' needs and the manager's criteria. If a particular software is pre-installed on the hardware that you intend to purchase, you should still list the software below. However, instead of indicating a price, you can state that it is pre-installed. Also, even if the software is freely available, it should be listed, with an indication that it is 'freeware'. You do not have to include drivers for hardware devices in your list. Any software that you intend to develop 'in-house' should also be costed by multiplying the hourly salary of the user who will develop the software with the total number of hours required for the development. If you intend to hire a programmer to develop the software, you need to include the hourly rate of the programmer.

URL:		
Software	**Specifications & Price**	**Justification**

URL:		
Software	**Specifications & Price**	**Justification**

URL:		
Software	**Specifications & Price**	**Justification**

URL:		
Software	**Specifications & Price**	**Justification**

URL:		
Software	**Specifications & Price**	**Justification**

URL:		
Software	**Specifications & Price**	**Justification**

URL:		
Software	**Specifications & Price**	**Justification**

You have now identified a set of possible software to be purchased/developed for your organisation. In the next section, you will consider the network infrastructure of the organisation.

Networks

Most organisations connect their computer systems in an internal network structure called a local area network (LAN) so that they can share resources such as databases and printers. A network structure requires specialised hardware and software to operate. You may have already considered this in the previous sections when discussing the hardware and software needs of your chosen organisation.

One of the most popular network architectures is the client/server architecture where the users' computers are clients interconnected in a LAN, that share processing tasks with one or more servers. In order to operate, a network requires a special type of operating system, as well as other network software. Some organisations develop and host their own websites on a web server, while others pay for their websites to be hosted by third parties.

Currently, there is no network in your organisation. As part of this module, you are required to propose the network infrastructure for your chosen organisation. This involves selecting the appropriate hardware and software to be acquired, if you decide that it is important to set up a LAN in your organisation.

Activity 2.6

Discuss the following questions with your project team. Where required, make assumptions about the organisation and/or the users if you do not have complete information.

1. Should a network be implemented in the organisation? Why or why not?
2. On what basis did you make your decision?
3. If you have decided to implement a network in the organisation, what hardware and software do you need to acquire?

Use the World Wide Web to search for specific network hardware devices and software, and the cost of acquiring it (if you haven't already done so previously). You do not need to consider any hardware or software for wide area networks (WANs), such as bridges, routers, gateways, etc.

As you work through Activity 2.6, make a note of the hardware and software that you come across and that may be appropriate (if you haven't done so previously). Also note the URL of any websites from where you sourced your information. Finally, justify why you have selected a particular hardware or software.

URL:		
Hardware/ Software	**Specifications & Price**	**Justification**

URL:		
Hardware/ Software	**Specifications & Price**	**Justification**

URL:		
Hardware/ Software	**Specifications & Price**	**Justification**

You have now identified the hardware and software needs of your chosen organisation, and investigated potential products to acquire in order to implement the IS/IT infrastructure. You have already been informed that the total budget for the infrastructure is $12,000. However, the manager must take out a loan for this amount, as the funds are not readily available. The manager has already approached several banks, all of which have different interest rates, and can arrange weekly, fortnightly or monthly repayments on either the full amount ($12,000) or on any other amount lower than that. The manager does not wish to take out a loan for more than one year. You are asked to prepare three sets of loan scenarios for the manager.

Activity 2.7

Using a spreadsheet package, prepare three sets of loan scenarios for the manager: one for weekly repayments, one for fortnightly repayments and one for monthly repayments on the following loan amounts: $8,000; $9,000; $10,000; $11,000 and $12,000, assuming that the interest rate varies from 5% per annum to 7% per annum with 0.5% increments (i.e. 5%, 5.5%, 6%, 6.5% and 7%). Each scenario should indicate the repayment for the different loan amounts and the different interest rates, so that the manager can look up a particular loan amount at a particular interest rate and determine exactly how much she/he would have to repay on a weekly basis, fortnightly basis or monthly basis.

Module 2 Outcome: IS/IT Infrastructure Plan

Module 2 consisted of activities designed to help you develop an IS/IT infrastructure plan for your organisation. By now, you should have a good idea about the hardware and software (including network hardware and software, if applicable) that the organisation requires to meet the needs of its users and that also satisfies the manager's criteria and constraints. You should have also realised by now that choosing the most appropriate hardware and software, and deciding how to purchase it, isn't a simple and straightforward task, especially for smaller organisations with limited resources!

Compile all of the information that you prepared based on the above activities into a single **IS/IT Infrastructure Plan** detailing all of the hardware and software that needs to be acquired and justifying each item in relation to the users' needs, as well as the manager's criteria/constraints. Use a spreadsheet to calculate the total cost of implementing your plan, bearing in mind that you have been given a budget of $12,000. Also, prepare relevant graphs to indicate at a glance how the majority of the budget is being spent. Finally, include the three loan scenarios to help the manager make a decision about how to finance the IS/IT infrastructure plan implementation. Your lecturer and/or tutor will provide you with information about how you should hand in/demonstrate your IS/IT Infrastructure Plan. You should also ensure that every member of your team has a copy of the plan.

Your lecturer and/or tutor will provide you with the marking criteria based on which your **IS/IT Infrastructure Plan** will be marked. Make sure you write down this criteria in the space provided below.

Marking Criteria	Marks
TOTAL	**100**

Reflection

Take a moment to reflect on the activities in Module 2. What did you think about the activities? What did you learn? How did your project team work together? Did you experience any difficulties? If so, how did you resolve them? What would you do differently next time?

Outstanding Issues

Do you have any questions that you would like to raise with your lecturer and/or tutor about the contents of this module? Use the space below to write them down.

Module 3

Organisational Database

Relevant lecture content	Data Management and Databases
Relevant textbook chapter(s)	
Due date	

Introduction

This module relates to the fourth component of an information system: data. Data are the building blocks of an information system, and as such data management is a critical function in all organisations. Data are stored in databases. As part of this module you will be required to design and develop an organisational database for your selected organisation.

Here is an outline of the tasks for this module:
- Define the organisation's data needs,
- Design a relational database for the organisation to support its needs,
- Select a database management system (DBMS) to implement the database,
- Develop a set of procedures for managing the database.

You will be required to use database management software as part of this module. Your lecturer and/or tutor will give you more information about this.

At the end of this module, you will be required to develop and submit an **Organisational Database** based on your work.

Database Design

Database design involves finding out what data an organisation requires to carry out its business activities and operations, and making decisions about how that data will be collected, stored, manipulated and used. This is the most important step in developing a database. Without an accurate understanding of the data that an organisation requires, it is not possible to develop reliable databases that employees and managers need to use in order to make important decisions. To develop reliable databases, the current *and future* data requirements need to be considered carefully. For example, an organisation may store data about its clients, all of who are currently based in Australia. As a result, they may decide not to store a client's country. Furthermore, since the postcode is an important piece of data, they may stipulate that the postcode is mandatory and must be stored for every client in the database. However, in the future, if the organisation expands by selling products online to overseas clients, it will not be possible to store the client's country. Furthermore, some countries do not have postcodes, yet the postcode is mandatory and must be stored. With some forward planning, the organisation could have avoided having to make changes to its database. This is why it is critical to carefully identify the data needs of an organisation.

Organisations store data about specific things or entities. For example, an **employee** is an entity about which an organisation will store the following data: name, address, phone number, date of birth and salary. Each business function requires data about certain entities. For example, the human resources function will need data about employees, however, sales and marketing do not need this data. They need data about a different set of entities (e.g. products, invoices, etc.).

Activity 3.1

Discuss the data needs of the organisation you have selected, with your project team. Consider the following issues:

1. What are the business functions that your organisation carries out? (e.g. human resources, sales, marketing, shipping, etc.)
2. Identify at least five different entities or things about which the organisation needs to store data (e.g. it needs to store data about **employees, customers**, …) in order to perform its business functions.
3. What data does the organisation need to store about each of those entities (e.g. employee name, employee address, etc.).
4. Prepare a matrix that shows what entities and corresponding data each business function requires (e.g. human resources will require data about employees, rosters, etc.).

Based on your discussion, complete the matrix below. An example is provided to help you. The entity is shown in **bold**. In the example below, both the Human Resources and Sales functions require the employee's name, however, only the Human Resources function requires the employee's other details.

List the entities and data here	List the business functions/activities here				
	(e.g. Human Resources)	(e.g. Sales)			
(e.g. *EMPLOYEE*					
Name	X	X			
Address	X				
Phone Number)	X				

A database consists of one or more interrelated tables. Each entity you have identified above, represents a table in your database. Each piece of data related to the entity is a field of that table. For example, the employee entity represents the EMPLOYEE table in your database, while the employee name, address and phone number are three fields in that table. Each row in the table is called a record. This structure is shown below, and is known as the relational model. The relational model is the most commonly used database structure.

EMPLOYEE TABLE

Employee Name	Employee Address	Employee Phone Number
Joel Smith	1 Smith St, Sydney 2000	(02) 111 11111
Li Ling	2 Ling Rd, Melbourne 3000	(03) 222 22222
Jane Brown	3 Brown Ave, Brisbane 4000	(07) 333 33333

Activity 3.2

Based on the data entities that you have identified in Activity 3.1, prepare a set of at least five tables for your organisation. Indicate the fields that each table consists of in the columns.

The relational model requires that each table have an identifier or primary key. The primary key field is needed in order to locate specific records. For example, if the EMPLOYEE table shown above contained the names of two employees who had the same first name and last name, it would not be possible to uniquely identify the record of one of those two employees. Therefore, it is necessary to set up a field that will uniquely identify a single record in the table – the primary key. In the EMPLOYEE table, the primary key could be the Employee ID, an identification number that is unique to each employee, as shown below. No two employees would have the same ID.

EMPLOYEE TABLE

Employee ID	Employee Name	Employee Address	Employee Phone Number	Employee Salary
11	Joel Smith	1 Smith St, Sydney 2000	(02) 111 11111	$45,000
22	Li Ling	2 Ling Rd, Melbourne 3000	(03) 222 22222	$48,000
33	Jane Brown	3 Brown Ave, Brisbane 4000	(07) 333 33333	$46,000

Activity 3.3

For each of the tables you identified in Activity 3.2, determine the primary key.

The primary key is also used to 'link' tables together. In the relational database, tables are linked through their primary keys. For example, while identifying your entities (and subsequently tables), you may have listed a sales entity with the following data: a sale ID, the ID of the product sold, the quantity of the product sold, the date of the sale and the ID of the employee who sold the product. We are keeping track of the ID of each employee that sold a particular product in order to pay him/her a commission. This entity is shown as a table below.

SALES TABLE

Sale ID	Product ID	Quantity	Date	Employee ID
ABC	123	500	12/12/2004	22
DEF	234	750	12/12/2004	22
GHI	234	700	13/12/2004	33
JKL	345	100	13/12/2004	22
MNO	345	520	14/12/2004	11

The primary key of the SALES table is Sale ID, while Employee ID is the primary key of the EMPLOYEE table. However, Employee ID is also stored in the SALES table for reasons described above. Therefore the two tables are *linked* through Employee ID. Where a primary key of one table is stored in another table, it is called a *foreign key*. So, Employee ID is the primary key in the EMPLOYEE table, and Employee ID is the foreign key in the SALES table. You should only link tables through a primary key and a corresponding foreign key. For example, you should not store the Employee Name (instead of the Employee ID) in the SALES table, because Employee Name is **not** a primary key!

Activity 3.4

Re-visit the tables you have identified in Activity 3.2 and the primary keys you have identified in Activity 3.3, and link the tables through their primary/foreign keys. Each table should be linked to at least one other table. You may have to make changes to your tables and fields in order to do this.

By now, you should have a set of tables, each with a unique primary key and other fields. Every field in the table, including the primary key, usually has different **properties**. For example, the Employee Name field will consist of alphanumeric characters (this is known as the *data type)* and may store up to 150 characters (some people have long names!). Other fields may be restricted to only certain values. For example, if all employees have an ID which is a two digit number, the Employee ID field should only accept numeric values up to 99. When two tables are linked through a primary key – foreign key, the properties of the primary key and the foreign key must be the same. For example, Employee ID in the EMPLOYEE table and Employee ID in the SALES table must both be numeric and have a length of 2 (i.e. store up to two digit numbers). If this is not the case, it may not be possible to link the two tables.

Activity 3.5

For each field in the tables you identified in Activity 3.4, specify the properties, including:
- the data type (numeric, alphanumeric, date, etc.)
- the length
- any restrictions on the values that can be entered into that field

Make sure that the properties for all primary keys which are also foreign keys match!

You have now designed your database which consists of a set of linked tables, each with a unique primary key. However, your tables are still 'empty' (i.e. there are no values stored in the tables). Entering values into a table is called *populating* the table. The EMPLOYEE and SALES tables above are populated with three records and five records, respectively. Populating tables is done through data entry using forms. A user will fill out a form, which is the interface that is used to enter and modify data in a database, and the data will be 'written' to the table. A user does not usually have access to the table itself, only the form. This is done for security and privacy reasons. A form does not have to contain all of the fields in a table.

For example, a form that is used to enter data into the EMPLOYEE table may not show the Employee Salary field, since this is private information that only certain individuals in the organisation will have access to.

Activity 3.6

Design a form interface for entering data into the tables you have created in Activity 3.5. Consider who will use each form, and based on that, decide what fields to include in your forms.

In addition to entering data into a table and making changes to the data, users also 'interrogate' the database. This is known as *querying* and involves finding answers to questions such as "Which employee had the highest sales in March 2004?" or "Where do the customers who bought product 123 between September 10 and October 9, 2004 live?". These are typical queries that a user (usually a manager) may pose to the database in order to make decisions such as which employees get a raise and where to advertise certain products. There is no limit on the number of queries a user may have.

Some queries are simple and can be looked up in a single table. For example, "What are the names of the employees who live in Sydney?" is a query that only requires the EMPLOYEE table. However, other queries are more complex and require the use of multiple tables to look up the data. For example, "What are the names of the products that Jane Brown sold in December 2004?". To solve this query, we need the SALES table where this data is stored. However, the SALES table does not contain the names of employees, only their ID. So first it is necessary to look up Jane Brown's ID in the EMPLOYEE table (which is 33 in the sample tables above). Once that's determined, the products that Employee ID 33 sold in December (only!) can be found in the SALES table (in our example above, that would be Product ID 234). However, the query requires the name of that product, not the ID, so presumably there would be a third table called PRODUCTS (with a primary key Product ID) which is linked to the SALES table through Product ID. Once the Product ID is found in the SALES table, the name of that product can be looked up in the PRODUCT table as shown below (in this case, it is a skirt).

PRODUCT TABLE

Product ID	Product Name	Price
123	T-shirt	$15.95
234	Skirt	$35.95
345	Trousers	$29.95

This is another reason why tables are linked through primary and foreign keys. The three sample tables above (EMPLOYEE, SALES, PRODUCT) are linked as shown below, which enables queries to be made on the data.

EMPLOYEE TABLE

Employee ID	Employee Name	Employee Address	Employee Phone Number	Employee Salary
11	Joel Smith	1 Smith St, Sydney 2000	(02) 111 11111	$45,000
22	Li Ling	2 Ling Rd, Melbourne 3000	(03) 222 22222	$48,000
33	Jane Brown	3 Brown Ave, Brisbane 4000	(07) 333 33333	$46,000

SALES TABLE

Sale ID	Product ID	Quantity	Date	Employee ID
ABC	123	500	12/12/2004	22
DEF	234	750	12/12/2004	22
GHI	234	700	13/12/2004	33
JKL	345	100	13/12/2004	22
MNO	345	520	14/12/2004	11

PRODUCT TABLE

Product ID	Product Name	Price
123	T-shirt	$15.95
234	Skirt	$35.95
345	Trousers	$29.95

Queries are usually generated using what is called Structured Query Language (SQL). However, this is generated automatically by most database software applications. The user only has to specify the fields and tables he/she wishes to include in the query, as well as any constraints (for example, we only wanted the *December* sales for Jane Brown), and the database software generates the SQL code which is then executed to give the user the results.

Activity 3.7

Discuss with your project team, what queries the manager of your selected organisation may wish to pose. Some typical queries that apply to most organisations have been provided as examples above. Think of others that would be useful and write them down. You should have at least six queries based on the tables you have developed, and at least four of those should be complex (i.e. require more than two linked tables to be solved).

Finally, most managers require a set of reports containing important summary information to make decisions. For example, managers will usually receive a Sales Report by Product or a Sales Report by Employee at the end of each week. Database software generates these reports for managers. To create a report, the user simply has to select the tables, fields or query results that are required and the software generates a summary report which can be sent to the manager or printed. A sample report based on the example above may look like this:

Sales Report by Employee
(December 2004)

Employee ID	Employee Name	Total Sales
11	Joel Smith	$15,574.00
22	Li Ling	$37,932.50
33	Jane Brown	$25.165.00

The total sales for this report were calculated by multiplying the quantity of each product that an employee sold with the price of the product.

Activity 3.8

Discuss with your project team, what reports the manager of your selected organisation may wish to receive on a regular basis. Consider the decisions that the manager of your organisation makes and use this information to guide your discussion. You should think of at least three reports based on the manager's needs and the tables you have developed.

You have now designed your database and decided which tables it will consist of, how the forms for entering data into the tables will look like, which queries users will make and which reports the manager will receive. You can now proceed to implement your database. This will involve actually creating the tables and forms, then populating the tables, and generating queries and reports. However, before your proceed with this, you still need to make some decisions about what database software will be used to implement it and how you will manage your database once it is implemented.

Database Implementation and Management

Database implementation involves physically implementing the database using database software or a database management system (DBMS) and making decisions about how the data will be physically stored.

There are a number of different database software or DBMSs available for a variety of users and organisations. One of the most popular DBMSs is the Oracle DBMS. However, every organisation needs to select an appropriate DBMS based on its available resources and needs. Some of the criteria that should be taken into account when making this decision include the following:

- the size of the database;
- the number of users who will use the database concurrently (i.e. at the same time);
- the DBMS features and how easy it is to use;
- the compatibility of the DBMS with existing hardware and software;
- the reliability of the DBMS;
- how widely the DBMS is used;
- the reputation of the software developer (supplier) and the availability of technical support;
- the cost of the DBMS.

Activity 3.9

Use the World Wide Web to do a search for database software (DBMSs) that is currently available. Select and evaluate three DBMSs and based on the information you have about your chosen organisation and the criteria above, make a recommendation about which DBMS to acquire. Justify your recommendation.

You may have already selected a DBMS in Module 2. If you have, re-visit your selection now that you have designed the database for your organisation and evaluated different DBMSs. Did you change your mind? Why or why not?

Use the space provided below to make notes as you work with your project team.

URL:		
DBMS Name	**Features, price & any additional info**	**Evaluation based on criteria**

URL:		
DBMS Name	**Features, price & any additional info**	**Evaluation based on criteria**

URL:		
DBMS Name	**Features, price & any additional info**	**Evaluation based on criteria**

Database management involves administering the database so that it remains useful to its users. It includes tasks such as preserving the integrity and accuracy of the data stored in the database, making back-ups of the database, and preventing unauthorised access.

Activity 3.10

Discuss the following questions with your project team in relation to your selected organisation and the database you have designed previously. You should use the World Wide Web and your textbook to find information to facilitate your discussion.

1. How will you ensure that the data stored in your database is valid, reliable and accurate? How will errors during data entry be prevented? How will the data be checked for inaccuracies?

2. How will you back-up your database? How often will you do this? Where will you store the back-ups?

3. How will you ensure that only authorised users have access to your database? Will everyone have the same level of access? Will you assign passwords to users? Will your database be available through the Internet?

Module 3 Outcome: Organisational Database

Module 3 consisted of activities designed to help you develop a database for your organisation. By now, you should have designed your database (tables, forms, queries and reports) and made some decisions about which DBMS to use to implement it and how to manage it after it is implemented.

Based on the activities in this module, you should now implement your **Organisational Database** using an appropriate DBMS. The DBMS may be the same as the one you have chosen as part of Activity 3.9, however, your lecturer and/or tutor may direct you to use a different DBMS which is available. When you have created your tables and set the primary key for each table, you should create the forms and then use these forms to populate your tables. Finally, you should implement the queries and reports that you specified previously. As you do this, you may find that some of the things you designed may not work as planned. You should make adjustments as necessary. Finally, write a one-page report to submit with your database that specifies which DBMS you have chosen and why, and how you will manage your database in relation to preserving the quality of the data, back-ups and preventing unauthorised access. Your lecturer and/or tutor will provide you with information about how you should hand in/demonstrate your database. You should also ensure that every member of your team has a copy of the database.

Your lecturer and/or tutor will provide you with the marking criteria based on which your **Organisational Database** will be marked. Make sure you write down this criteria in the space provided below.

Marking Criteria	Marks
TOTAL	**100**

Reflection

Take a moment to reflect on the activities in Module 3. What did you think about the activities? What did you learn? How did your project team work together? Did you experience any difficulties? If so, how did you resolve them? What would you do differently next time?

Outstanding Issues

Do you have any questions that you would like to raise with your lecturer and/or tutor about the contents of this module? Use the space below to write them down.

Module 4

Web-Based Information System

Relevant lecture content	Web development, web-based information systems and e-commerce
Relevant textbook chapter(s)	
Due date	

Introduction

This module relates to the use of the Internet and the World Wide Web to support business growth and development. Most businesses today have a presence on the Web either through a full web-based information system that can handle business transactions with clients, suppliers and other business partners (usually referred to as e-commerce or e-business systems) or a more simple system in the form of a website which provides information about products and services. As part of this module you will be required to design and develop a web-based information system for your selected organisation.

Here is an outline of the tasks for this module:
- Discuss the purpose of the web-based system and the different stakeholders and their needs,
- Design a web-based information system to meet the needs of the stakeholders,
- Make a decision about hosting arrangements for the web-based information system,
- Develop a set or procedures for ongoing management of the web-based information system.

You will be required to use web development software as part of this module. Your lecturer and/or tutor will give you more information about this.

At the end of this module, you will be required to develop and submit a **Web-based Information System** based on your work.

Web Design

Designing a web-based information system is a complex task that requires organisations to carefully examine their needs and goals, as well as other stakeholders' needs and goals. Unlike internal information systems that are used by employees only, a web-based information system is an external system that is accessed and used by a variety of stakeholders, including clients and potential clients, suppliers, business partners, government entities, etc. As such, the web-based information system serves a number of different purposes and must cater to the needs of a diverse group, while still helping the organisation achieve its goals. To design an effective web-based information system, careful planning must first be undertaken.

The first question that an organisation must address is whether it actually requires a web presence at that point in time. Although most organisations today take for granted that a web presence is essential, this must be balanced against the resources invested in designing and developing an *effective* web presence. Once the organisation has established whether it requires a web presence and whether it has sufficient resources to design and develop an effective web-based information system, the planning process begins by determining what purpose the web presence will serve. Is it intended to be a marketing and promotional tool? Will clients be able to place orders for products? Is it intended to cut costs by providing information and resources online to clients?

Activity 4.1

You have decided that the organisation you selected requires a web-based information system. Discuss the purpose of this system with your project team. What will the web-based information system do? What will it provide to your organisation's stakeholders? What will it do for your organisation?

Based on your discussion above, indicate the purpose of your web-based information system in the space below.

The purpose of the web-based information system is to:

-
-
-
-
-
-

The next step involves identifying the stakeholders who will use the web-based information system. It is important to define these stakeholders in relation to their needs and goals, as well as other characteristics such as demographics, their experience with computers and the Web, their interests, etc. Building a thorough understanding of your stakeholders will help you target them more effectively. It is also important to consider how and why a particular stakeholder group is identified. While some stakeholders are obvious (e.g. clients and suppliers), others may not be so apparent. For example, you may find out that research students are using your web-based information system to carry out research about Internet use and usability.

Activity 4.2

Discuss who the stakeholders of the web-based information system are, with your project team. Consider issues such as their needs and goals, their background (if known), their computer and Web experience (if known), and any other characteristics or interests. Where required, make assumptions if you do not have complete information. You should also note how/why you identified each particular group of stakeholders.

Write down the key points arising from your discussion in the space provided below.

Stakeholder Group	Needs/Goals	Other Characteristics	How/Why Identified

Having defined the purpose of the web-based information system and the stakeholders and their needs, it is now necessary to begin thinking about the system itself. In other words, what will the system do (*functionality*) or what information will the system contain (*content*) that will serve its purpose AND meet the needs/goals of the stakeholders. Some typical functions that a web-based information system might provide to stakeholders include searching, ordering (shopping carts), payments and credit card processing, tracking orders, feedback forms, events calendars, membership applications, chat rooms, discussion boards, polling, directories, online help, etc. The content on web-based information systems can vary widely and can include information about the organisation, its products and services, its clients, etc.

Activity 4.3

Discuss the functionality and content requirements for each of the different stakeholder groups you have identified in Activity 4.2, with your project team. Think about the different functions and content that each group will find useful to satisfy their needs and goals and consider how these will be useful to the stakeholders.

Write down the key points arising from your discussion in the space provided below.

Stakeholder Group	Functions	Content

The results of your previous discussion will give you a good idea about the level of complexity of your web-based information system. A simple website which mainly provides information to stakeholders, and minimal functionality is 'quick and easy' to implement, while complex e-commerce systems that include ordering and transaction processing functionality are time-consuming to develop and require thorough evaluation and testing.

It is now time to consider how you will structure the functions and content that you have identified. A web-based information system consists of hyperlinked web pages. The way these pages are organised will affect how easily the system users can navigate through the system. Users should be able to build a 'mental map' of the system quickly and easily if the structure is logical and flexible. This means that users will find the information they need without 'getting lost', but at the same time, be able to navigate to different pages without the need to begin from the starting page (or *home page*) every time.

The structure of a web-based system is best depicted using a diagram with the home page at the highest level and all the other pages at lower levels. Although the diagram usually has a hierarchical structure, it should also indicate any hyperlinks *between* pages at lower levels as well as any other direct hyperlinks that do not conform to a hierarchical structure. A sample diagram is shown below.

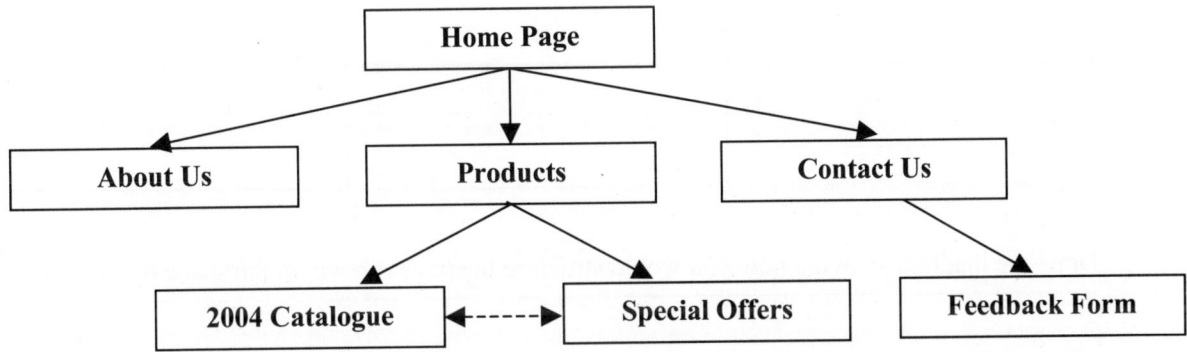

Activity 4.4

Discuss how you will structure the functions and content that you have identified in Activity 4.3, with your project team. This involves making decisions about what functions/content to include on each web page and how many pages to have. Once you have decided this, draw a diagram to show how your web pages will be structured.

Use the space provided below to specify what functions and content you would place on each page.

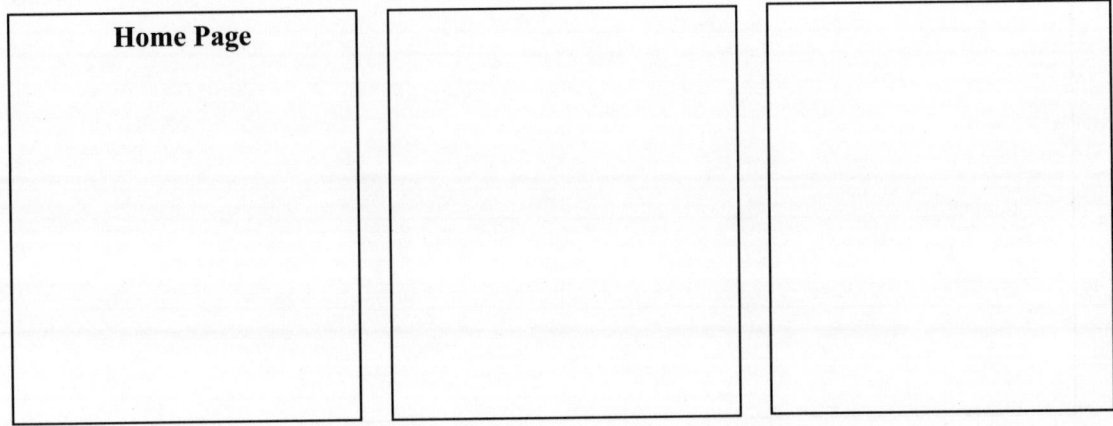

Draw the diagram showing how you would structure the pages above, in the space below.

You have now designed your web-based information system conceptually and can proceed to implement it. This will involve actually developing the system using a web development software tool. However, before you proceed with this, you still need to make some decisions about how you will 'host' your system and how you will manage it once it is implemented.

Web Hosting and Management

Before you implement a web-based information system, you must decide how and where you will 'host' it. Most organisations have a web server to do this, however, small businesses often don't have the technical expertise and resources to maintain a web server. They usually pay a third party to host the system for them.

Activity 4.5

Discuss with your project team how you will host the web system that you have designed. Will you purchase a web server for your organisation and do you have sufficient funds to do this? You may have already specified a web server in Module 2 as part of the IS/IT Infrastructure Plan. If not, you should find out what web servers are available.

If you are planning to have a third party host your system, do a search on the Web to find out what they offer and how much it costs. Remember that some companies only offer limited space to host a web system so if your system is complex, you will need to take that into account.

If you are going to have a third party host your web system, use the space provided below to make notes as you work with your project team.

URL:		
Company	**What they offer**	**How much it costs**

URL:		
Company	**What they offer**	**How much it costs**

URL:		
Company	**What they offer**	**How much it costs**

URL:		
Company	**What they offer**	**How much it costs**

Managing your web-based system once it is implemented involves things like updating content and content management, technical support, implementing security mechanisms, checking usage statistics, and evaluating the system to find out if it continues to be useful to the stakeholders.

Activity 4.6

Discuss the following questions with your project team in relation to managing your web-based system. You should use the World Wide Web and your textbook to find information to facilitate your discussion.

1. How will you update the content on your website? Who will do this? How often? How will your users know that the content has been updated?
2. How will you check that that your system is up to date and contains no 'broken' links?
3. Who will provide technical support for your system in case of problems?
4. What security mechanisms will you implement to protect your web system (e.g. a firewall)?
5. What types of usage statistics will you collect for your system and how will you use these?
6. How will you evaluate your web system to ensure that it is useful and user friendly? How often will you do this?

Module 4 Outcome: Web-Based Information System

Module 4 consisted of activities designed to help you develop a web-based information system for your organisation. By now, you should have designed your system (i.e. decided what functions and content to include and how to structure it) and made some decisions about how to implement it and how to manage it after it is implemented.

Based on the activities in this module, you should now implement your **Web-Based Information System** using an appropriate web development software tool based on your design. Create each page of your system and link the pages so that users can navigate through it. If you have included some complex functions in your system (such as ordering and credit card payments) you do not have to implement these so that they actually work. You should only show how they would look. For example, you can create a product ordering form, but it doesn't actually have to place an order. Finally, write a one-page report to submit with your system that specifies your hosting arrangements and justification as to why these arrangements are the most appropriate for your organisation, and how you will manage your system in relation to the following:

- Content management
- Technical support
- Security
- Usage statistics
- Evaluation

Your lecturer and/or tutor will provide you with information about how you should hand in/demonstrate your system. You should also ensure that every member of your team has a copy of the system.

Your lecturer and/or tutor will provide you with the marking criteria based on which your **Web-Based Information System** will be marked. Make sure you write down this criteria in the space provided below.

Marking Criteria	Marks
TOTAL	**100**

Reflection

Take a moment to reflect on the activities in Module 4. What did you think about the activities? What did you learn? How did your project team work together? Did you experience any difficulties? If so, how did you resolve them? What would you do differently next time?

Outstanding Issues

Do you have any questions that you would like to raise with your lecturer and/or tutor about the contents of this module? Use the space below to write them down.

Module 5

IS/IT Management Plan

Relevant lecture content	Types of information systems; Systems development; Strategic IS management; Contingency planning
Relevant textbook chapter(s)	
Due date	

Introduction

This module relates to the planning and strategic management of information systems and technology in organisations. Most organisations use a variety of information systems (some of which are integrated), and new ones are developed on a regular basis. Managing these systems is essential to ensure that they support the organisation's business activities and operations effectively and efficiently. As part of this module you will be required to prepare an IS/IT management plan for your selected organisation.

Here is an outline of the tasks for this module:
- Discuss the different types of information systems your organisation needs,
- Consider how you would develop the system and whether you would outsource it,
- Determine the strategic role of the system and any external factors that affect it,
- Develop a set of contingency plans to protect your system.

You will be required to use word processing software as part of this module. Your lecturer and/or tutor will give you more information about this.

At the end of this module, you will be required to develop and submit an **IS/IT Management Plan** based on your work.

Types of Information Systems

There are a variety of different information systems (e.g. transaction processing systems, management information systems, decision support systems, etc.) that support the work and activities of employees at all levels in an organisation. You are most likely familiar with these systems by now, having discussed them in lectures. You will now consider some of these systems in relation to the organisation you have selected for this project.

Activity 5.1

Discuss whether the organisation you have selected would require any of the following types of systems currently or in the future, and, if so, indicate which ones and how/why they would be used:

- Transaction processing systems
- Management information systems
- Decision support systems
- Executive information systems
- Expert (knowledge-based) systems

In your discussion, you should take into account any of the above systems that currently exist in the organisation. Keep in mind the goals and size of the selected organisation!

Use the space below to make notes during your discussion.

	Is it required? Why?
Transaction processing systems	
Management information systems	
Decision support systems	
Executive information systems	
Expert (knowledge-based) systems	

More than likely, you have identified some systems that do not exist in the organisation. You will now consider the design and development of these systems.

Systems Design and Development

Systems design and development is a complex activity undertaken to build information systems. The most well known method for building a new system is called the Systems Development Life Cycle (SDLC). You are most likely familiar with the SDLC by now, having discussed it in lectures. The SDLC consists of a series of steps that are followed to design and develop a new information system. These steps include:

- Analysis
- Design
- Implementation
- Maintenance.

During Analysis information is gathered about any existing information systems, as well as the users' needs. This is done in order to define the requirements for the new system and involves analysing existing documents, conducting interviews with users, etc. Naturally, a lot of data and information is collected during Analysis and sometimes Computer Aided Software Engineering (CASE) tools are used to store and manage this data.

Activity 5.2

You have decided that it is necessary to design and develop one of the systems that you identified in Activity 5.1. Choose any system and discuss with your project team how you would collect information about the new system requirements. What techniques would you use? How would you keep track of the system requirements? Would you use CASE tools? Why or why not?

After the Analysis, the system is designed based on the specified requirements and then implemented. Implementation involves generating the programming code, testing this code, hardware and software installation, building databases and testing amongst other things. The final, ongoing step, involves maintaining the system.

One of the decisions that has to be made during the SDLC is whether to outsource any of the design and development. Sometimes organisations may not have the resources to develop systems 'in-house' and they may find it cheaper to subcontract this process to another organisation. This is known as outsourcing.

Activity 5.3

Discuss with your project team whether you would outsource any of the system design and development in your selected organisation, in relation to the system you chose in Activity 5.2. Explain your decision providing arguments for and against outsourcing, based on your selected organisation and its needs.

Strategic IS Management

Information systems are not developed and do not exist in isolation. In order to provide the organisation with a competitive edge, they must fit in with the overall business strategy and support the long-term business goals and objectives. For example, if the business strategy is to provide low-costs products, the information systems should assist with cost reductions that can then be passed on to customers.

Activity 5.4

Read through the mission and goals of your selected organisation. Discuss with your project team whether the system you have chosen to develop in Activity 5.2 supports the organisation's mission and goals. How does it do this?

The impact of any external factors on information systems must also be well understood. The legal, political and competitive environments can all have a significant effect on information systems. For example, when the GST was introduced in Australia, all financial information systems had to be modified to reflect these changes.

Activity 5.5

Discuss with your project team which external factors can impact the system you have chosen to develop in Activity 5.2. How would they impact the system and to what extent? What can you do to reduce any negative impacts?

The impact of some external factors can be catastrophic for an organisation. For example, a fire could destroy all of the organisation's information systems and data. The final section of this module will examine issues related to contingency planning in order to minimise the damage caused by such catastrophic events.

Contingency Planning

Business continuity or contingency planning is a 'must' for organisations, yet many still do not have a plan of action in case of a catastrophe such as natural disaster. An organisation cannot operate without functional information systems. Imagine a bank that loses all of its clients' records and financial information! Contingency planning usually involves developing different situation scenarios and then deciding on an appropriate course of action if a situation occurs.

Activity 5.6

Discuss with your project team how you would protect the system you have chosen to develop in Activity 5.2 in each of the following situations:
- A flood
- A hacker has broken into your systems and destroyed some of your data
- A computer virus

Discuss specific measures you would take to minimise the likelihood of the situation occurring in the first place, as well as the corrective measures you would take in the aftermath.

Module 5 Outcome: IS/IT Management Plan

Module 4 consisted of activities designed to help you develop an IS/IT management plan for your organisation. By now, you should have discussed various aspects of building and managing information systems that support the strategic goals of your organisation.

Compile <u>all</u> of the information that you prepared based on the above activities into a single **IS/IT Management Plan** detailing which new system you would develop, how you plan to collect the requirements for the new system, whether you will outsource, how the system will support your business strategy, what external factors will have an impact on the system and how you plan to protect your system in case of a flood, hacking and a virus. Your plan should be professionally presented using a word processing software. You should also prepare a mail out to all your clients (you may have already got their names and addresses in Module 3 if you created a client or customer table) so that each client receives a letter and a copy of the report. The letter should explain what the report is about and ask for feedback. Your lecturer and/or tutor will provide you with information about how you should hand in/demonstrate your IS/IT Management Plan. You should also ensure that every member of your team has a copy of the plan

Your lecturer and/or tutor will provide you with the marking criteria based on which your **IS/IT Management Plan** will be marked. Make sure you write down this criteria in the space provided below.

Marking Criteria	Marks
TOTAL	**100**

Reflection

Take a moment to reflect on the activities in Module 5. What did you think about the activities? What did you learn? How did your project team work together? Did you experience any difficulties? If so, how did you resolve them? What would you do differently next time?

Outstanding Issues

Do you have any questions that you would like to raise with your lecturer and/or tutor about the contents of this module? Use the space below to write them down.